Written by Monica Perez

Illustrated in the style of H. A. Rey by Mary O'Keefe Young

HOUGHTON MIFFLIN HARCOURT
Boston New York 2011

For Brian Lee Perez, with love
—M.P.

For Matthew, my shining star
—M.O'K.Y.

www.hmhbooks.com

www.curiousgeorge.com

The text of this book is set in Adobe Garamond.

The illustrations are watercolor.

Library of Congress Cataloging-in-Publication Data is on file.

HC ISBN 978-0-547-24284-2

PA ISBN 978-0-547-24285-9

Manufactured in Mexico

RDT 10 9 8 7 6 5 4

4500403250

George was a good little monkey and always very curious.

One hot afternoon he heard, *Jingle-jingle. Jingle-jingle.* What could that music be? George was curious about the melody he heard coming in through the window.

“That’s an ice cream truck, George,” said the man with the yellow hat. “You know summertime is here when you start hearing the music of the ice cream truck.”

George loved trucks, and he loved ice cream. Ice cream would taste so good on a hot day like today! He would find this wonderful ice cream truck right away. He started to climb out the window, but his friend stopped him. George had to finish his lunch first.

By the time George rushed out the door, the music was gone.

"Don't worry, George," the man said. "The ice cream truck makes a trip around town each day, all summer long. We'll catch the ice cream truck tomorrow."

The next day it got hotter and hotter. George waited for the ice cream truck, but there was no sight or sound of it.

“Let’s go to the pool, George,” said the man with the yellow hat. George ran to get his towel. Splashing around in the pool would be a great way to beat the heat!

But the pool was closed for renovation.
"Look on the bright side, George. By autumn, we'll have a larger pool with three diving boards. Won't that be fun?"
It did sound fun. But George needed to cool off now, not in the autumn!

So, George went back to waiting for the ice cream truck. He dreamed of vanilla, chocolate, and strawberry ice cream bars.

George thought he heard the music of the ice cream truck once . . .

. . . but it was just a little boy's harmonica.

George and his neighbors decided to go to the park to run through the sprinklers. But just as they arrived, the sprinklers were turned off.

It was a long walk back home. Luckily for George, there was lemonade waiting for him on the porch.

George took a drink and made a face. It was warm.

"Sorry, George," the man with the yellow hat said. "Our freezer has decided to stop working. All our ice cubes have melted."

Now would be the perfect time to hear the sweet sound of the ice cream truck. Wait—was that it? Yes, there was the truck turning the corner now!

"Wave it down, George. I'll be right back with my wallet!" The man rushed back into the house.

But the ice cream truck driver could not see the little monkey on the curb. The truck was not driving very quickly, but it was driving away!

George looked back at his house.
He looked at the truck.

Then he had an idea.

George climbed a tree

and swung
from branch

to branch

until he swung right onto
the roof of the truck.

He rode the truck into town.
The truck stopped beside the
town park.

A window on the side opened up, and a small child and her mother stopped to buy ice cream.

George could not believe his eyes. The little girl had ordered a frozen treat that looked exactly like a chocolate-covered banana! George danced happily. He knew exactly what to order. The little girl saw him and laughed.

So many people wanted ice cream that the driver ran out of change. He hurried over to the nearby bank to get more.

Meanwhile, George noticed that the ice cream line was getting very long. Everyone looked hot. There was no shade to stand in. Maybe he could help.

George jumped down into the truck, where it was dark and cool. He grabbed as many ice cream bars, cones, and ice pops as he could. He handed them out to the waiting children, their parents . . . and even their pets!

George worked so quickly, he didn't remember to collect money for the ice cream. No one seemed to mind—except the ice cream man!

"What have you done?" he cried when he returned. "Half my ice cream is gone!" George climbed up a telephone pole. George was very glad to see his friend hurrying toward the park.

"Hold on a minute," said a voice below. "Look at how everyone is enjoying themselves! It's been the hottest summer in town history. An ice cream social is exactly what we need."

It was the mayor, and she offered to pay for everyone's ice cream. "Thank you, George, for your great idea. I think the town should sponsor an ice cream party every summer!"

The ice cream truck driver was happy to keep serving ice cream. George and the man with the yellow hat helped.

The ice cream man saved one last treat for George—
a chocolate-covered banana-cicle! Delicious!